D0581744

ESSEX
GIRLS

ESSEX GIRLS

For Profane and Opinionated Women Everywhere

Sarah Perry

First published in Great Britain in 2020 by
Serpent's Tail,
an imprint of Profile Books Ltd
29 Cloth Fair
London EC1A 7JQ
www.serpentstail.com

Copyright © Aldwinter Ltd

1 3 5 7 9 10 8 6 4 2

Typeset in Elena by MacGuru Ltd
Printed and bound in Great Britain by Clays Ltd, Elcograf S.p.A.

A CIP catalogue record for this book is
available from the British Library.

ISBN 978 1 78816 745 1
eISBN 978 1 78283 821 0
Audio ISBN 978 1 78283 829 6

For my sisters

As I write this, I cannot but wonder when and
how you will read it,
and whether it will cause a single throb at the
idea that
it may be meant for you.

Harriet Martineau, *Life in the Sick-Room: Essays*, 1844

1

EARLY ONE EVENING some months ago, I returned by bus to the town where I was born, and alighting in Chelmsford at a stop on Wood Street I found myself attended by Essex ghosts. Some distance from where I stood, I saw a red brick wall stained by efflorescence and surmounted by black iron railings. Behind the wall, beyond a length of grass, I saw for the first time a row of modern houses, which had been built since I last visited. Standing in the dusk, the bus departing behind me, I could read this wall like a manuscript. It is all that remains of the hospital where I was born weeks early in the autumn, not having been expected until winter: I was blue, my father tells me, and a shocking sight. The hospital was demolished thirty years after my birth, and had by then been empty and derelict for years. In a photograph taken before the demolition and published in the local press, a black iron fire escape extends up the exterior wall of a forbidding building, and vegetation is rampant at the windows; it is just possible to make out the white chimney of the hospital incinerator beyond the pediment. On the tarmac, which is cracking open in the carpark, a solitary chair has been abandoned, as if an anxious patient has just departed the waiting room.

But I knew this wall was a palimpsest, so I went on reading, and found – beneath the corridors down which my mother had walked with me in her arms – the Chelmsford Union Workhouse, whose fourteen rooms and infectious ward became the St John's Hospital; and behind the workhouse an almshouse, which was 'always wanting repair'; and behind this the barracks that stood on that same ground. Then I thought

St John's Hospital, Chelmsford, shortly
before its demolition in 2010.

I saw, in the passages that ran between the modern houses, the dead remnants of an Essex past still going about their business: Hetty Alderson, for example, who in 1893 was sent at the age of fifteen from the workhouse to be employed and beaten by the wife of a cycle manufacturer, and coming up behind her, farm boys from Prittlewell and Steeple, too thin for their scarlet regimental tunics.

Then – I was in no hurry, and the evening was pleasantly dark – I saw, passing without effort through the wall and iron railings, the ghosts of three Essex girls coming out to greet me. First came Rose Allin, with her head wrapped in a length of cloth, and a jug of water in her right hand: she was young and walking briskly, and had in the folds of her dress the scent of burning wood. Then bustling little Anne Knight, with her piercing pale eyes, holding up a white sign, and gesturing fiercely to it: Chelmsford was her home town, and she hadn't come far. Then – after a minute or two, and with an apologetic air, since she was an Essex girl not by birth, but by temperament – Emily Hobhouse, concealing a slight cough in a fine lawn handkerchief.

As I saw them there, I recalled how late I had come to feminism, and how each of these women had in their way formed my sense of myself as a feminist. I suppose I am not alone in having once been oblivious to what I owed to women before me, and to the notion that I ought to find ways of repaying the debt. I had not been raised to see any inequity between the genders, still less to deplore it; and if I thought of feminists at all, it was with a vague sense of a militant effort which had once been a necessity and was now mercifully redundant. It did not occur to me that the 'Essex girl' joke which I inhabited was a feminist matter, and that I ought to interrogate and challenge it. Later, and by small degrees – by dint of speaking with women, and reading women, and listening to women; by understanding that if I felt I'd slipped through life without encountering misogyny's knocks and slights, this was in large part owing to the comfort and privileges of my life and identity – I came to understand that I should cultivate and harden my feminism for my own sake, perhaps, but largely for the sake of other women.

In her essay 'Men Explain Things to Me', Rebecca Solnit says of the feminist project:

> That so much change has been made in four or five decades is amazing; that everything is not permanently, definitively, irrevocably changed is not a sign of failure. A woman goes walking down a thousand-mile road. Twenty minutes after she steps forth, they proclaim that she still has 999 miles to go and will never get anywhere.

These three ghosts set out early on the thousand-mile road, and I'm afraid I joined them rather late; but it is because of their company I've come to believe that it is a matter of pride, and not of embarrassment or shame, to be called an Essex girl.

2

LEFT TO MY OWN DEVICES, I might have given little thought to the county where I was born, and its various regional ghosts. My Britishness seems to me largely an administrative matter, and I'd no more think to be proud of my Englishness than of my fingernails or feet; but the fact that I'm an Essex girl has been more difficult to evade or deny. As a child and teenager, when visiting towns in other counties or arriving in 1998 at the polytechnic in Cambridge where I studied English, I was asked where I came from or where I lived, and would find my response met with a knowing smile. *An Essex girl*, they'd say, laughing, and look me up and down for evidence, in the manner of a witch-finder seeking a suspicious wart: *I see*. It seems curious to me now that it was never necessary to ask what it was they meant. I understood without explanation that an Essex girl was a contemptible thing, if not absolutely beyond a sort of mocking affection. She was blonde, but not naturally so, and if her clothes altered with the fashion of the years they altered only slightly, and were always designed to display a body that rested precisely on the boundary between desirability and repulsion. She wore leopard print; she wore stiletto heels; she was not stupid exactly, but devoted what intellect she had to the acquisition of sexual partners and the ramshackle care of innumerable squabbling children. She was certainly not educated, nor did she wish to be. She lived in council housing – I felt I was to understand that this, too, was a mortal sin – and when she danced, which was often, she danced around her handbag. This handbag was white patent leather, and from the rear-view mirror of her car she hung fluffy pink dice.

She was called Tracy, or possibly Sharon; she was all appetite. Anne Boleyn had spent a good deal of time in Essex, and this probably explained her scheming rapacious behaviour, her determination to get her man. 'Essex girls usually come in twos,' wrote Germaine Greer in the *Guardian* in 2001, with a relish that betrays a kind of contempt, 'both behind pushchairs with large infants in them ... The Essex girl is tough, loud, vulgar and unashamed ... when she and her mates descend upon Southend for a rave, even the bouncers grow pale.' The idea of the Essex girl has been so broadly accepted, and so deeply embedded in the British psyche, that in 1999 the *British Medical Journal* published the article 'Are there excess Sharons in genitourinary clinics?'. 'Are those "Essex girls" Tracey, Sandra and Sharon really women of easy virtue?', researchers wondered, and set about totting up the names of patients – the female ones, mind you – attending a sexual health clinic in Southampton over a calendar year, concluding that 'the much maligned' Essex girls were seen 'half as often as expected' (by a considerable margin the most commonly seen name was, in fact, Sarah). The Essex girl has become a useful repository for a score of social anxieties: an irredeemably vulgar, plump, sexually threatening, feckless and indolent woman, an affront to morality, and a threat to the values of sobriety, industry and obedience that prop up the ruling class – she is 'anarchy on stilts', wrote Greer. At the girls' school I attended, we occasionally wondered what it meant to be an Essex girl, and could make little sense of it – though I confess that on the last day of school even the most industrious of girls could be found standing on the pavements outside and flashing their breasts at passing motorists. We were not all white, for example, which seemed to be a requirement (despite its proximity to London, Essex does not particularly benefit from ethnic diversity, with less than 6 per cent of its population identifying as Black or minority ethnic in the 2011 Census; though

in 1908, at the Kursaal in Southend, a Senegalese woman called Princess Dinubolu
took part in a beauty competition, having
been barred from entry in Great Yarmouth,
on account of her 'light chocolate' skin'.[i] Mr
Bacon at the Kursaal had warned her by tel-
egram not to take part: 'Don't enter. Local
prejudice.'). Some of us were working class,
and others owned a horse or two, and looked
as if they might stand to inherit their grandmother's pearls. If, by sixth form, a number
of students had become thrillingly glamorous and sexually active, those same students
returned to school and applied themselves
to physics or Latin. Besides, so what if they
had not? There is nothing particularly moral
about an A Level. I was by no means sophis-
ticated enough to understand that it was a
luxury to stand aside and look at the concept
of the Essex girl with a sort of detached
confusion, and that in fact it indicated a profound and pernicious degree of misogyny
and snobbery. No woman wants to be seen
by a sexual-health clinician who believes

her forename indicative of anything but her parents' taste.

Still: I was an Essex girl, and there was nothing I could do about that. In the Old English of Saxon Essex, *stede* means 'place', and so I was steadfast: held to the place of my birth. And was there ever less persuasive an ambassador for her county? Brought up devoutly Christian, I wore modest skirts and dresses which I made myself, and which reached to the floor, so that it was often said of me that I moved not on legs, but on castors. The name 'Sharon' suggested to me not a libertine harridan half-cut on cheap white wine, but the rose of Sharon in the Song of Solomon. I did not wear the stilettos I was assured were the mark of my tribe, but my father's old Scout boots; I'd never danced, either around a handbag or away from one; I was blonde, but in a dark unremarkable fashion; a childhood passed largely in chapel and at home had smoothed my Essex accent down to the occasional glottal stop; and though I daresay I might have cultivated an energetic sexual freedom under other circumstances, I married at twenty, having settled on my husband at thirteen. So I dispensed with Essex altogether, and if I ever thought of the county of my birth, I peopled it not with the brassy vulgarians I'd concluded were nothing to do with me, but with the ghosts that had attended my birth: the faces in the workhouse window; the women in the leper colony down at Moulsham, where in due course I went to buy paint and paper for my homework; the Saxon king buried with a hoard of gold in a field in Prittlewell. I was occasionally reminded of my Essex identity when the reality show *The Only Way Is Essex* became popular, and on those occasions I suppose I laughingly affirmed the distinction between myself and those gleaming, tanned young people and their hectic, half-real and half-fabulated lives. I moved away, and what remained of my accent was hidden – or so I hoped – behind a fair imitation of a Radio 4 continuity announcer, unless I was particularly amused or annoyed.[ii] The idea of the Essex girl – which was always part joke, part myth – receded from my view. In my case it was merely an irritation, not a form of oppression, and it would have been quite absurd to feel more than faintly piqued when, as a white, straight woman of considerable privilege, it was all nothing but a glancing blow.

But in recent years, my native accent asserting itself, I have been turning back to Essex and its women. I cannot quite account for it, except to think that I am looking for my tribe. It is not that I have ever been lonely, but I have always felt alone: the solitary occupant of my category of one. It seemed to me that by dispensing with the idea of the Essex girl altogether, out of a kind of confused and snobbish disdain, I had cast myself out of a community of women that might otherwise have welcomed me in, and conferred on me an identity. 'Anarchy on stilts', Germaine Greer had said; and so I wondered if after all there was something pleasingly anti-establishment about the Essex girl. Might a woman who shrugs off the demands of respectability and a nicely guarded reputation be intrinsically radical? It struck me that Gemma Collins – the grande dame of *The Only Way Is Essex*, in whose big, beautiful and superbly glamorous person every Essex girl trope is exemplified – had achieved a kind of sleight of hand, by taking society's contempt, packaging it in leopard-print silk, and selling it back at a profit. What a thoroughly and admirably disreputable thing to do!

In *A Vindication of the Rights of Women*, Mary Wollestonecraft devoted a chapter to the subject of 'Morality Undermined by Sexual Notions of the Importance of a Good Reputation', and wrote:

It has long since occurred to me, that advice respecting behaviour, and all the various modes of preserving a good reputation, which have been so strenuously inculcated on the female world, were specious poisons ... The leading principles which run through all my disquisitions, would render it unnecessary to enlarge on this subject, if a constant attention to keep the varnish of the character fresh, and in good condition, were not often inculcated as the sum total of female duty ...

What is an Essex girl, if not a woman who cares nothing at all for a good reputation? I began to understand that perhaps she was feared and despised because, having rejected one female duty, she was better equipped to reject them all.

3

IN 2016, the *Wall Street Journal* published an advertisement which supported the denial of the mass slaughter of the Armenians which had taken place a century before. I had been researching this genocide for the novel I was working on at the time, and was particularly drawn to the women that bore witness to the events, such as the nurse Ruth Parmelee, who wrote of the outrages that 'they were too harrowing to try to describe'. On seeing the advertisement in the *Wall Street Journal*, a remarkable woman of Armenian heritage came forward and continued to bear witness. A successful businesswoman, she put her wealth and influence to use, and taking out a full page advertisement in the

New York Times, wrote: 'In 1939, a week before the Nazi invasion of Poland, Hitler said: "Who, after all, speaks today of the annihilation of the Armenians?" We do. We must.' In 2018, towards the end of May, dressed in sombre black clothing concealing her body from neck to wrist, this same woman met the President of the United States to plead clemency for Alice Marie Johnson, a 63-year-old Black woman serving a life sentence on non-violent drugs charges. The meeting took place on the incarcerated woman's birthday; some days later, her sentence commuted, she was released.

I suppose if you were to picture to yourself this black-clad woman, pleading the case for social justice, you might easily enough furnish her with her voice, her demeanour, her clothing: a slight, determined person, perhaps, worn down by ambition and board meetings, or a formidable bluestocking accustomed to commanding a room with a deep stentorian voice. But this in fact is Kim Kardashian, the reality TV star whose fame began with a pornographic videotape released, as she said in court, against her will; whose body is perhaps more scrutinised, desired and despised than that of any other woman today; who arrived at the Met Gala in 2019 in a corseted latex dress designed to give the impression of dripping nudity.

I invoke her here because she is the Essex girl elevated to her purest form, displaced from Southend to Los Angeles: hyper-sexualised, irredeemably vulgar, a body presented to an avid and insatiable male gaze in a fashion which is somehow both gratifying and confronting; materialistic in a manner which can only repulse, when set against the economic and social inequalities that split the country of her birth; given to intricate and voluble familial squabbles, and adopting a manner of speech which is irritating to the ruling classes. The Essex girl is not bound by geography, but is a type, metonymous for a very particular kind of female agency, and a very particular kind of disdain: she contains a multitude of women.

Kardashian came again to my mind as I prepared to deliver a lecture which is held in Norwich each year in commemoration of Harriet Martineau, who had been born in the city in 1802. I had decided I would ask Martineau to walk out of Norfolk, to cross Suffolk without pausing, and to join me in the county of my birth: I wanted to introduce her to my Essex ghosts, and make the claim that she too had been, in her way, an Essex girl. Martineau was prone to illness all her life, and having lost her sense of taste and smell as a child was, by her late teens, so hearing impaired that she adopted the use of an immense ear trumpet (this object being weaponised later in life, when it would be withdrawn from use during conversations which bored or exasperated her).

At the age of twenty-seven, her family having become impecunious after the failure of their textile business, she began earning a living by publishing articles, and went on to produce a number of books on subjects including political economy and

Harriet Martineau, aged 54, shown at her needlework
in a photograph by Moses Bowness, 1855–56.

mesmerism. She was of a radical political bent, and by the 1830s had become a feted figure in London's political circles. Matthew Arnold wrote of her that 'no man of a certain delicacy of intellectual organisation' could fail to have a just appreciation of her, and while more or less confined to her rooms by sickness (which in due course was cured, she said, by mesmerism and the application of magnets to the body) she wrote a biography of the Haitian slave rebellion leader Toussaint L'Ouverture, and several books for children. She advocated passionately for matters which remain both urgent and unresolved: for sustainable living and adequate and compassionate hospital provision, for racial equality and for the rights of women. She collaborated with Florence Nightingale, and was a friend to Dorothy and William Wordsworth, and to the Arnolds, and – though not always entirely happily – to George Eliot, of whose elopement with a married man she thoroughly disapproved.[iii] In her collection of essays *Life in the Sick-Room*, she shows an acute engagement with the effects of chronic illness, and writes out of her own sick-room into those of women and men that she has never met, and will never meet, proposing a kind of secret communion of suffering:

> At all events, there is something sweet and consoling in the fellowship. Though we would, if we could, endure anything to set the other free ... yet, as this cannot be, we may make the most of the comfort of our companionship. In our wakeful night seasons, when the healthy and the happy are asleep, we may call to each other from our retreats, to know each how the other fares; and ... it may be that there are angels abroad ... who may bear our mutual greetings, and drop them on their rounds.

There is a humanistic quality to her work on suffering which anticipates a modern sensibility, and in fact she was a confirmed and practising atheist (in December 1850 Matthew Arnold wrote that he had 'talked to Miss Martineau (who blasphemes frightfully)'). In 1851, she published *Letters on the Laws of Man's Nature and Development*, in which she corresponded with Henry Atkinson, and together they more or less ridiculed conventional Christianity and the Genesis Record fully eight years prior to the publication of Darwin's *On the Origin of Species*.

But it is not easy for a woman to secure a lasting reputation, since this seems to me to be as much predicated on being liked and respected by peers, and by being assessed against a series of subtle and punitive social norms, as on her work. After the publication of Martineau's correspondence with Atkinson, it was felt she had been duped by his malign influence, since certainly no mere woman could arrive at so anarchic a position as atheism on her own account. It was a 'humiliating inversion of the natural order', wrote her brother, after which he never saw or heard from her again.

On her death in 1876, Harriet Martineau – to the last a devotee of scientific inquiry and progress – offered both her brain and her ears as specimens for dissection and study: both were politely declined. Historians have declined also to make much of her reputation and her work,[iv] and not always politely. In *The Victorians*, A. N. Wilson writes waspishly that her works were 'wordy and cliché-ridden', and accused her of having 'all the right views – that is the views espoused by the metropolitan intelligentsia' (as if being inquiring and educated, and living in an immense city drawing its citizens from all over the world, makes a woman less equipped to remark on current affairs, and not more). Dickens meanwhile wrote sardonically that she was 'grimly bent upon the enlightenment of mankind' – an ambition which would likely have been met with praise and not with censure had it been attributed to a man.

How to account for this diminution in her reputation? It seems to me to have been in some ways a matter of a failure to conform to what is expected – now as then – of a woman. In old age, Martineau – living by then in the Lake District – scandalised locals by wearing hobnail boots and smoking cigars. She professed no great interest in romantic attachments, so that some commentators have wondered if in fact she was a lesbian, perhaps because to contemporary sensibilities this is both more palatable and more credible than her simply having been more a creature of intellect than of romance. Nathanial Hawthorne wrote of her that she was 'a large, robust (one might almost say bouncing) elderly woman, very coarse of aspect, and plainly dressed … And this woman is an Atheist, and thinks, I believe, that the principle of life will become extinct, when her great, fat, well-to-do body is laid in the grave.'

I suppose there were never two less likely companions than these two women. On the one hand we have Kardashian, whose brand was described in the *New Yorker* as being predicated on the possession of 'a perfect (and perfectly unaffordable) female body'; on the other a talkative, intelligent, plain woman, fat, disabled and chronically ill, and heedless of the need to make herself attractive and agreeable to men. But were they to have joined me that evening in Chelmsford, beside the hospital wall where my Essex ghosts assembled – Martineau in fifteen yards of black bombazine; Kardashian in a corseted dress which will not permit her to sit down – I am minded to think they might have exchanged a nod of mutual recognition, and even perhaps of approval.

4

HAVING SET ASIDE my prejudice, and beginning to conceive of the Essex girl as a kind of radical that I could admire and emulate, I went in search of her origins. I'd fondly imagined myself to have been subject to an ancient insult, made noble by long use; that this unapologetic, recklessly embodied and irrepressible woman must be a geographical archetype, particular to those 1,420 square, flat miles stuck between London and the sea. In AD 60 Roman Colchester had been razed to the ground by a vengeful red-haired Boudicca, and reduced to nothing but a reddish stratum of dust and ashes, studded with pottery shards, beneath the modern town. In fact she was Queen of the Iceni, in neighbouring East Anglia; but all the same, it was pleasing to think that Essex became at that moment a site where women ransacked the obligations of their gender. I wondered if the women of Essex had always been more than usually subject to a half-desiring, half-damning male gaze, and was amused to discover that Samuel Pepys, finding himself in the town of Saffron Walden late in the winter of 1660, soundly kissed the inn-keeper's daughter ('she being very pretty'), and then moved on to Epping, where he had 'merry talk with a plain bold maid', this a pithy distillation of the qualities of an Essex girl. According to Herbert W. Tompkins and his *Companion into Essex*, there was once in Widford a pub called The Good Woman, as if such a creature is as rarely seen in the county as a white hart or a red lion: the inn sign depicted a headless woman, since the only truly good woman is one without a voice.

I have sometimes heard it said that if there is an Essex girl origin myth, it can be

found in the embers of the Jacobean witch
trials: I saw Goody Proctor in stiletto heels.
Despite my natural bent towards either the
Puritanical or the rational, I'm not myself
above the use of Tarot cards, and so was
delighted at the thought that as an Essex girl
I might be suspected – if only ever unconsciously – of pacts with the devil, and of
being in possession of arcane powers. The
citizens of Essex were particularly familiar
with the pricking-pin and the ducking-stool,
and the Witchfinder General Matthew Hopkins[v] – though himself a Suffolk man – lived
in Manningtree on the River Stour, where
in 1647 he overheard a group of women dis-
cussing their meeting with the devil, and so
realised his vocation.

In the first-person accounts of Essex
assizes where women were tried, I imagined that I would find accusations levied
at women because they'd shown a disin-
clination to Christian worship, or because
they had been open and free with their
sexual desires, or because they had been

Matthew Hopkins with witches and
their familiars, from the frontispiece to
Hopkins's *The Discovery of Witches*, 1647.

menopausal, or simply elected to live beyond the bounds of the town in whitewashed cottages, dispensing tinctures of chamomile flower or valerian root. But I discovered – not without disappointment – that suspicion would light on a woman for the most banal of reasons: a stolen glove, for example, or the failure to repay an insignificant loan. If, as I imagine, more subtle motives moved the accusing finger, I never found mention of them; rather, it seemed that petty irritations, and feuds which had festered between neighbours for years, found their expression in the violent and unholy collaboration of church and state. In *A Detection of Damnable Driftes*, an account of the trial of three women accused of witchcraft in Chelmsford in 1579, we find one Elizabeth Frances confessing to having gone to her neighbour asking for a loan to buy yeast . On being sent away empty-handed, she encountered on the road 'a Spirit of white colour seeming like to a little rugged Dogge', with which she entered into a bargain in exchange not for her soul, but for a crust of white bread. What I discovered in these accounts was not defiant women who had stepped beyond a boundary and been punished for it, in whose exquisite torments I could take a kind of spurious relish, but rather the small irritations of small communities, exacerbated by poverty, superstition and a theocratic state, metastasising into a fatal social disease.

If I had hoped to dignify the Essex girl by reason of her great age, I failed. I am the youngest of five daughters, and if we were not all born in Essex we were certainly raised there, and so I consulted my sisters. Had they, too, found the idea of the Essex girl trailing them – a shadow clicking in her white high heels – down the corridors of school and into their places of work? The oldest two of my sisters disavowed this absolutely: it had simply never come up. The third sister thought perhaps it had been said once or twice; the fourth, who is closest to me in age, had shared my sensation that I was followed about by a being I didn't recognise but could never shake off. Consulting the Oxford English Dictionary, I found its first use dated to 1991; though the Google NGRAM tool, which scans an immense catalogue of published information for words and phrases, shows a precipitous increase in the phrase from 1989. So the modern notion of the Essex girl is more or less a construction of the Thatcherite era, and useful because she can sustain a kicking from both sides of the political field. For those of a conservative bent, her intemperate behaviour and supposed dependence on the state makes her a useful cautionary tale; for those on the left, her materialism and vulgarity seem revoltingly capitalist.

In the village of Wrabness, a few miles along the River Stour from where Matthew Hopkins retired, there stands The Essex House. This is a monument to the Essex girl raised by the artist Grayson Perry, himself a kind of Essex girl by virtue of his birth and of his alter ego Clare. It is a gaudy and marvellous construction out of all keeping with the faintly rising fields, as if on the Essex land did Kubla Khan a stately garden shed decree. Its extravagant interior of timber panelling, tapestries and tiling constitutes one immense artwork in commemoration of the life of Julie Cope, a fictitious woman born on Canvey Island in 1953, in the year of the great North Sea flood, and whose career as a social worker was abruptly halted when she was fatally struck by a curry delivery scooter on Colchester High Street. It is, said the artist, 'a monument to thwarted female intelligence', and if there's deliberate bathos in the means of her death there is a sincere and evident fondness in each tapestry stitch. (Asked if he felt the brassy construction with its harlequin tiles was appropriate to the banks of the River Stour, Grayson Perry, with laughing disbelief, said 'Appropriate? That's not a word I really worry about.')

The Essex House is an extraordinary tribute to an ordinary woman, but my Essex girl isn't there. I wanted to think she was herself extraordinary: to believe that it was possible to seize the pejorative and make it an aspiration. Her bad reputation relates to a particular kind of visible and confronting female agency, hinging on a flagrant disregard for the establishment, and a willingness to place her personal freedoms above public approval. If it is the case that the personal is political, then to adopt modes of dress which are mocked, and to speak in an accent which is not the accent of the ruling classes, and to care nothing for the 'specious poison' of a chaste reputation, constitutes a radical political act. So I do not want to say: the Essex girl is not vulgar, does not revel in wealth and belongings, is modest, educated, intelligent and polite, and worthy of a good reputation. I want instead to say: rejecting modesty and respectability demands an exercise of personal liberty which is essentially anti-establishment, and which has always attracted a degree of censure.

5

THE GHOST OF ROSE ALLIN – water jug in hand – first attached herself to me when I was a child. The Chelmsford chapel I attended arranged a summer camp each year in Suffolk, and one afternoon, having crossed the boundary back into Essex, we visited the village of Great Bentley. Its sign promises a site of complacent, postcard Englishness: a pheasant in his country tweeds observes a hay cart; a man in white takes a wicket. Together with a handful of other children and the adults taking charge, I crossed the village green – which, as its residents will tell you, is the largest in the country – and sat cross-legged on the grass. After we'd sung grace, I suppose to the amusement of anyone passing by, we ate our sandwiches; and then one of the men handed each child a small pink leaflet. On the cover, in firm black lines, was a drawing of a woman's hand held over a candle, and in large letters the name ROSE ALLIN. I knew her story and her name, and had seen this image before, but never so enlarged: I almost thought by some transmission of suffering through the paper I could feel the flame on my skin. Then I was asked to read the leaflet aloud – I was a precocious child, and never much minded being heard to speak – and so I did, wondering sometimes if the village and its visitors were perplexed by this peculiar small crowd with their sung grace, and the child in her long dress reading from a sheet of pink paper. And though it is not in the least in keeping with the teachings of the chapel who brought her to me, I sometimes think that afternoon I summoned up Rose Allin, and that her spirit has never left my side.

She was born in 1537, in what was then

known as Much Bentley. She lived with her mother Alice Mount, and her stepfather William, and hers was a Protestant family – a happy enough theological and social position under the reign of King Edward VI, who affirmed and amplified the new theology which his father Henry VIII had effectively caused to be law. But in 1553 the king suffered a disease of the lung, and a dreadful swelling in his legs, and having whispered to his tutor 'I am glad to die', departed the throne. It was occupied then by Mary Tudor, whose avid determination to overturn the Reformation and return England to the fold of the Catholic Church caused Rose Allin and her family to become, more or less overnight, traitors to the crown by virtue of their religion.

On 7 March 1557, which was the first Sunday in Lent, and at two o'clock in the morning, Rose and her family were woken by one Master Edmund Tyrrell. He brought with him a Bailiff of the Hundred, and two local constables. Perhaps the family had been indiscreet at worship, or had been the subject of local gossip; but whatever the cause, they were to be questioned for practising their faith in a manner which was not only illegal, but which, if considered tantamount to treason, carried the penalty of death.

Alice Mount at that time was ill, and Rose asked if she might be given permission to fetch her a drink of water. As she returned – carrying in one hand a jug and in the other a candlestick – she was stopped by Master Tyrrell. Possibly a young woman of twenty, caring for her mother and with her body and soul equally imperilled, might have aroused his sympathy; at any rate he set about chastising her for her faith. She ought really to be a good Catholic, he said – and I daresay the chiding, paternal tone of a man to a woman who really ought to know better echoes quite unchanged down the years – and called her 'a gossip'. The penalty for a girl who insisted on treasonous practices such as the use of the Bible in English was, he reminded her, that she should be tied to a stake and burned alive. Then, as if it would hardly be possible for her to properly fear such an ending without material evidence of the forthcoming pain, he took from her the candlestick she was holding, gripped her by the wrist, and passed the flame over the back of her hand in the shape of a cross, until – so it was later said – 'the very sinews cracked asunder'.

Rose was taken with her family to Colchester, and imprisoned in the castle built on the ground which Boudicca had laid waste. To a visiting friend, she said, 'While my one hand was a burning, I, having a pot in my other hand, might have laid him on the face with it, if I had would; for no man held my hand to let me therein. But, I thank God, with all my heart, I did it not.' But I would not like you to think that Rose was compliant, or that she lacked courage. She had the capacity for impertinence and anger, and on being asked her opinion of the seven Catholic sacraments retorted with

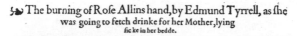

The burning of Rose Allins hand, by Edmund Tyrrell, as she
was going to fetch drinke for her Mother, lying
sicke in her bedde.

Rose Allin's arrest, from an engraving in
John Foxe's *Acts and Monuments*.

marvellous Essex girl vulgarity that they 'stank in the face of God'. Having been despatched soon after back to her cell, she was heard to be singing. Then, on 7 August 1557, at some time between six and seven in the morning, Rose Allin – an Essex girl just out of her teens, whom nobody could persuade that any man or any authority had the power to make her act against her conscience and her will – was taken to piece of hard ground by Colchester's city wall, tied to a stake with her mother and her stepfather, and burned alive.

As a child on Great Bentley village green, I handed back the leaflet from which I'd read aloud, and was conscious of some alteration in my mind. I'd been brought up in a chapel which was led by men, and directed by men, and I was taught to cover my hair when I worshipped, because this was a sign of deference both to men and to God. From that chapel pulpit and in those chapel pews only men were ever heard to pray, or to speak, or to read aloud from the Bible; I was, I'd been led to understand, not precisely an inferior being by virtue of my gender, but certainly a different one, and that difference required me to be obedient to men, and to hold my tongue in church. It was not that I lacked for girls and women to admire – my mother, for example, was a maths teacher, and had taught herself to read Russian while bringing up her five daughters; and chief among my Biblical favourites were the prostitute Rahab, who lied to save the skin of some Israelite spies, and Jael, who slaughtered a military leader by driving a tent-peg clean through his skull – but that I'd been born a girl seemed to me a profound misfortune. I was taller and stronger than the few boys I knew, and if not cleverer I certainly thought I was: was I really to be pliant, and acquiescent, when this ran so counter to my nature? I looked at the drawing of Rose Allin's hand held above the candle, and thought that perhaps after all I needn't always do as I was told.

The account of Rose's martyrdom is taken

from the work of John Foxe, whose *Acts and Monuments of these Latter and Perilous Days, Touching Matters of the Church* is commonly known as the *Book of Martyrs* (though Foxe himself protested this bowdlerised version of the original sonorous title, declaring that he wrote 'no such booke'). This work, now relegated to the interests of historians and specialists, has done as much as any other work of literature to shape the English consciousness.[vi] Foxe had himself been a devout Protestant, and having fled England for the continent during the persecutions under Mary Tudor, he returned to find, according to his records, 312 Protestant men, women and children dead, because they had been burned at the stake, or hanged, or had died in prison. Among these had been his friends and peers, and since he had already been at work on an account of Christian martyrdom from the days of the Roman Empire, he set about collating accounts of the arrest, interrogation, torture, trial and martyrdom of the English Protestants, in due course publishing the first edition in 1563. This consisted of a single volume too heavy and too immense to be held in one hand, and was by far the largest book yet to be produced in English. It contained 60 woodcuts depicting the torments of the martyrs, and described their sufferings in florid detail, down to the particularities of burning flesh, so that we read how John Hooper, for example, 'knocked his breast with his hands, until one of his arms fell off, then knocked still with the other, what time the fat, water and blood dropped out at his fingers' ends'. Its success was immediate, prompting Foxe to produce a second and greatly expanded edition in 1570, this running to two volumes, and 2,300 folio pages.

The source of its appeal is not particularly difficult to discern. Leaving aside all that it could offer the ghoulish, it resembles as a work of narrative nothing so much as *The Canterbury Tales*. Its pages are thickly populated with villainy, and its heroes are drawn as much from the gutter as from high office.

There are episodes of the most extraordinary pathos, and reversals of fortune which would make a novelist blush: consider, for example, the moment the deposed Archbishop Cranmer holds out the hand with which he signed his recantation, and lets it burn first in the fire. To the court of Elizabeth I, for whom no blackening of her predecessor's name could have been sooty enough, it was a gift. In its way, the book played a part in what in due course became the persecution of the English Catholics – man, as has always been his habit, handing misery on to man.

But it is necessary to apply a pinch of Maldon sea salt to the *Book of Martyrs*. Foxe, a bereaved man who had passed years in fear of his life, permitted his bitter loathing of the Catholic Church to permeate each narrative. That the book had been co-opted by the political interests of the royal court was evident in its evolving title; readers of the second edition were informed that these were 'tumults styred up by Romish Prelates in the Church'. Foxe responded to accusations of exaggerated or falsified testimony by either deluging the accuser with masses of corroborating information, or – if persuaded of his error – discreetly removing the contested account.

Still: I am not inclined to look entirely askance at the story of Rose Allin, and let her spirit depart from me. She has grown more precious to me in the intervening years, not less. I had met her first in my father's study, when I was perhaps six or seven years old, kneeling down by the shelves, and taking out his eighteenth-century edition of Foxe, and holding it open on my lap because it was too heavy for me to carry. In the woodcut illustration she is a plump girl with a delicate foot extending from under her skirts, and a water jug held loosely; as Master Tyrrell attends carefully to her hand with the candle, her face seems resolute to me, and in another room her father is kneeling by her mother's bed. So when I met her again on the Great Bentley village green I was meeting an old companion, and if she passed from view for a time, she returned to me as I sought out my Essex girls. What I have come to understand is that the Protestant martyrs of the sixteenth century were not only men and women of an unswerving religious conviction, but that they were also political radicals.

It is difficult to comprehend the magnitude of Rose Allin's defiance without first grasping the significance not only of her desire to worship as her conscience directed, but to read the Bible in English, an act which was itself an offence. The King James Bible – battered copies of which may be bought by the dozen in any high street charity shop, at the cost of a pound or two – is a radical political text. It represents an act of dissent against an oppressive state, furnishing ordinary men and women with the means to equip themselves with a degree of knowledge which had been until then the preserve of the ruling classes – and it has always been in the interests of an oppressive government to keep the people in a state of ignorance.[vii] If, as Marx says, the history of all hitherto existing society is the history of class struggles, then the struggle of the Protestant martyrs was a matter of class. In a letter to Bishop Bonner – who came to be called Butcher Bonner for the enthusiasm with which he pursued dissenters to the pyre – one inquisitor spoke repeatedly of the heretics as 'poor, ignorant wretches', and among them we find illiterate women, butcher's boys and tradesmen, weavers, shoemakers, and a blind child. In *Godless Morality: Keeping Religion Out of Ethics*, Richard Holloway writes:

> The great traditions have all had their casualties, of course ... Women and children were probably the ones who paid the highest price, since they have always been the ones who were most vulnerable to the abusive power of the systems that enclosed them.

When the Bishop of London discovered that copies of Tyndale's New Testament in English were smuggled across the Channel in wine barrels, he burned them on the steps of St Paul's. The depth and profundity of Rose Allin's faith, and the idea that a mere abstraction held value higher than her own life, is beyond comprehension to the contemporary secular imagination, but hers is not only a quaint tale of antique self-abnegation. She remains an animating force, and a reminder that one need not be particularly equipped with education or status to set one's face against injustice. Solitary acts may seem to count for nothing against whatever engines of state or structure grind down the collective and the individual, but radical political acts need not be of the scale or type that results in a memorial on a village green.

If Rose Allin these days would pass unnoticed and unoppressed – a white girl and a Christian, irritated perhaps by the mockery of her birthplace, but no more – for oppressed communities the mere act of existence is radical. The Black poet and philosopher Audre Lorde – who identified herself as 'a dyke', defusing and empowering the pejorative by adopting it, and whose *Cancer Journals* share a sensibility with Martineau's *Life in the Sick-Room* – wrote: 'Caring for myself is not self-indulgence. It is self-preservation, and that is an act of political warfare.'

6

IN JUNE 1840, in London's Exeter Hall, the British and Foreign Anti-Slavery Society held the World Abolition Conference, and devoted much of the first day's proceedings not to the question of the emancipation of enslaved people, but to whether or not women should be permitted to attend as delegates. The official report of the convention notes that in the end 'the upper end and one side of the room were appropriated to the ladies, of whom a considerable number were present'. When Benjamin Robert Haydon completed his painting commemorating the event the following year – positioning the abolitionist and emancipated slave Henry Beckford in the centre of the foreground

– he included, towards the far right of the immense canvas, a group of six women, and among them, in a lace-edged bonnet, was the Essex girl Anne Knight.

She was in fact a Chelmsford girl, born to a grocer in 1786. She was a Quaker, which was and remains in its way a radical identity, with a commitment to equality, peace and social justice being more a less a tenet of the faith. In 1825, she joined the Chelmsford Ladies Anti-Slavery Society, and – being fluent in both German and French – travelled Europe in the company of other Quaker women, attending to various charitable causes: a Grand Tour for the politically conscious.[viii] She was an indefatigable correspondent, covering sheets of paper in a large and looping scrawl, and something of a difficult dinner guest, on occasion wearing a silk bag attached to her belt, and reaching into it to withdraw pamphlets should she encounter a political opponent in need of correction and reproof. Deploring the treatment of women by the leaders of the

Chartist movement, she wrote with brisk disfavour that for them 'the class struggle took precedence over women's rights'. Writing of the inability of women to vote in national elections (at that time women of a certain financial standing could vote in local political elections), she said: 'I am forbidden to vote for the man who inflicts the laws I am compelled to obey – the taxes I am compelled to pay – taxation without representation is tyranny.' Notwithstanding the urgency with which she felt her disenfranchisement, it is vital to understand that she did not define the nature of her womanhood by the ways in which that nature was repressed. She did not so much chafe against the constraints of her gender, as refuse to feel the constriction: 'We are not the same beings as fifty years ago;' she said: 'no longer "sit by the fire and spin", or distil rosemary and lavender for poor neighbours.' That conventional womanhood prevented her peers from doing their duty as citizens infuriated her: when her friend Maria Chapman was unable to attend the abolition conference, she bemoaned the other woman's married state, which had doubtless led to her absenting herself from the cause of justice. 'Ah, that thou hadst not married!' she wrote. 'That thy "proper sphere" at this juncture should have been nature's recess instead of reason's exercise! Ah me!' She favoured in particular the immediate and not the gradual abolition of slavery, and was a friend and confidante of her fellow abolitionist Elizabeth Heyrick, who understood that slavery was a stain on the collective white conscience (Heyrick wrote, 'The perpetuation of slavery in our West India colonies is not an abstract question, to be settled between the government and the planters; it is one in which we are all implicated, we are all guilty of supporting and perpetuating slavery'). Together with Heyrick, Knight had been a founding member in 1824 of what became the Female Society of Birmingham, a women-led abolitionist movement that favoured action such as a sugar boycott above protestation alone (and meanwhile in the United States, three Black sisters – Margaretta, Sarah and Harriet Forten – excluded from their national abolitionist movements because of their gender as Anne Knight was excluded from hers, founded the Philadelphia Female Anti-Slavery Society, which operated from 1833 until 1870, after the Fourteenth and Fifteenth Amendments granted all citizens born in the US, at any rate in theory, equal rights).

Knight was a splendid publicist for her various causes, producing coloured labels printed with slogans, designed to be fixed to the envelopes in which her letters and pamphlets were circulated. And in 1847, when an anonymous broadside appeared, it was agreed by those familiar with her distinctive tone to have been the work of Anne Knight, and is now widely regarded as the first pamphlet on women's suffrage. 'NEVER', said the pamphlet's author, 'will the nations of the earth be well governed, until both sexes, as well as all parties, are fully represented and have an influence, a voice, and a hand in the enactment and administration of the laws.'

I lived for eighteen years in the town where Anne Knight was born, and never heard her name. The fault of course must partly be mine: a few yards from Chelmsford railway station there is an austere grey building which is the former Quaker Meeting House, and which bears her name on a blue plaque, but I never thought to look. I found her by chance, as I set about raising the ghosts of Essex girls to accompany Harriet Martineau, and what I saw of her first was not her pamphlets, or the immense and idiosyncratic store of her correspondence, but a photograph of her in old age. It depicts a woman whose white braided hair is concealed by a black bonnet, and whose rather strange pale eyes are narrowed in apparent scrutiny. She is dressed in an immense quantity of stiff black clothing fastened with buttons, and in her gloved hands she is holding a placard. On this placard is written, in a sloping copperplate, 'By tortured Millions – By the

Divine Redeemer – Enfranchise Humanity – Bid the Outraged World – BE FREE'.

What caught and held my gaze was the significance of a woman already elderly by the mid part of the nineteenth century so strenuously declaring her radical politics. The photograph suggests a lifetime's labour, affirming the vitality and presence of women in the political sphere for the full duration of the century, and earlier. It has become a habit to conceive of women – both historically and currently – not by their achievements, but by the restraints placed upon them; to study the locked door, and fail to see the windows broken from inside. This characterisation constitutes a kind of silencing, which has a very particular effect. If it is commonly believed that women departed home and hearth in the early twentieth century, importunately demanding the vote, as if the Suffragists hatched out of an egg which had been incubated by the heat of the Great War, then the continuing demand for equal rights – including, and in fact particularly,

Anne Knight, aged 69, with her placard.
Photographed by Victor Franck in 1855.

for marginalised women – seems a kind of modern phenomenon. Understand what a long march it has been, and you may demand sight of the destination far sooner.

When I first met Anne Knight, it had been two years since the publication of my second novel, which was set in the late nineteenth century. In it, I had depicted two women typical of the age: educated, politically astute Londoners, sociable and gregarious, at liberty to travel, to work, to desire and be desired. I was astonished to find that these women were repeatedly described, both by critics and by readers, as ahead of their time: 'strong women', as the saying goes, as if such a thing is both unusual and contemporaneous. Much was made of apparent anachronisms: they moved about without chaperones, for example, and addressed each other by their first names; they held intimate friendships with men. So it has become a habit of mine to say, whenever the opportunity presents itself, that no, this is not quite right: that these were nineteenth-century women as the evidence paints them. In the town of Wormingford in Essex in 1807, women held office in the positions of churchwarden, overseer, surveyor and constable; in 1865 Elizabeth Garrett Anderson passed the Society of Apothecaries examinations, and eleven years later an Act of Parliament was passed allowing women to enter the medical profession. In 1869 the first female students were admitted to Cambridge, at the newly opened Girton College; here Hertha Marks Ayrton read maths, going on to become an expert in electricity, and to become, in 1899, the first female member of the Institution of Electrical Engineers. When uplifting the voices of these women, I am often met with the reproving suggestion that these are merely outliers, remarkable more for their rarity than for their achievements and their lives. But this reproof carries with it the suggestion that they were not merely untypical for women of their time, but untypical for women at all, and so I refute it, not without annoyance, where I see it.

Even where it is accepted that women have historically taken a vital and active role in politics and social justice, the caveat is often entered to the effect that this was the preserve of the privileged few: a social conscience as a form of *noblesse oblige*; qualms for those who could afford them. In this way the voices of women are diminished; and the voices of poor women and women of colour are diminished still further. But in 1843, women in the parish of St Chad's in Lichfield cast their votes for an official in a local election, and among them were a dressmaker, a pauper, a servant and a washerwoman. In 1888, at the Bryant and May match factory in East London, women and teenaged girls – working there under conditions which caused injuries from which they could never hope to recover – went on strike, having undertaken sustained industrial action for two decades, including a march on the Houses of Parliament involving up to 10,000 girls and women (with the assistance of the activist Annie Besant, they secured improved working conditions, and the strike came to an end). And at the beginning of the twentieth century, Indian women – Lolita Roy, for example, who became President of the London Indian Union Society, and who marched under an appliqued banner with Bhagwati Bhola Nauth and her daughter – were part of the movement for women's suffrage.

So Anne Knight holds up her placard, and fixes the dubious observer with her pale unblinking eyes. 'Woman has the capacity for *instructing man*', she wrote, and her toils 'have strengthened her mind and matured her judgment till she is now *superior* to man ...'

7

IN THE WEST SUSSEX coastal village of East Wittering, in the early days of 1926, a woman of sixty-six lived with her maid Ella in a damp cottage from which she was able to hear the coming and departing tides. Her home was a sick-room, so that she might well have found consolation in the company of Harriet Martineau and Audre Lorde; and she wrote to her friend Tibbie Steyn:

> All the morning as the slow dawn crept on, I have lain listening to the long melancholy moaning of the sea as the waves break upon the shingly shore. It seemed as if daylight and Ella would never come. Yet tonight thank Heaven I had no pain

or cough but only the weakness which often seems to me worse than pain. To raise myself in bed becomes an effort and I can no longer get up, light my stove and make my coffee as I want.

In a photograph taken towards the end of her life, she is a small, delicate person, aged beyond her years. She wears a fur coat against the cold, and a style of bonnet which is long out of fashion; her thin hands are clasped in her lap. Her eyes are deeply set, and with a melancholy perceptive quality: she looks steadily out at the observer. She is – or at any rate she seems to be – the epitome of a fading spinster caught between the wars, bearing her small sufferings with a genteel fortitude, and unsuited to any climate beyond the cottage doors.

This frail woman in her winter furs is Emily Hobhouse, who once wrote of herself that 'pens won't adequately tell all I have seen and done'. She is not, I confess, an Essex girl, except in spirit; but a Cornishwoman, born in 1860 to an upper-middle-class family, a daughter of the Archdeacon of Bodmin, and a gentlewoman. The first three decades of her life were passed in a fashion which was not untypical of an intelligent and comfortably off Victorian girl with an acute social conscience. She worked diligently with her father for the good of the Parish poor: she founded a library; she walked great distances;[ix] she tended to minor ailments by dispensing herbal remedies, having consulted her grandmother's books. Since her mother died when she was twenty, and her father was in generally poor health, her ambitions and intellect were for much of her youth confined more or less to the domestic sphere.

With the death of her father, Emily was conferred a degree of freedom which she seized at once, and with a determination entirely in keeping with her character; and in 1895 she sailed for New York. She wrote to her sister, 'I feel as if I were in fairyland, or the Arabian Nights.' On to Minnesota then,

Emily Hobhouse, aged 42, photographed
by Henry Walter Barnett in 1902.

where Cornish miners were set to work and, she felt, doubtless in need of support and encouragement from a fellow countrywoman: here she opened a library, and founded a choir, and sang to patients in the hospital. All this was met with disfavour by men: an episcopal minister – mindful of the same Biblical strictures which had required me, as a child, to cover my hair in chapel, and never to be heard in services unless I was singing – took her to one side, and subjected her to an hour's lecture on her spiritual faults (and here, I think, the ghost of Rose Allin is concealing a smile). 'He did not think', wrote Emily, 'that St Paul would approve of my holiday mission services in a log camp. I said I should do it all the same.' She was acquiring a bad reputation: nevertheless, she persisted.

She returned to England in 1898, having become engaged, bought a Mexican ranch, broke off her engagement, and lost most of her fortune in bad speculations. A year later, with the outbreak of the Boer War, she was invited by a Liberal MP to serve as the secretary for the women's branch of the South African Conciliation Committee. Her concern was not with the fortunes of the British army, but rather with the 'enemy' women. She wrote, 'it was late in the summer of 1900 that I first learnt of the hundreds of Boer women that become impoverished and were left ragged by our military operations.' Favouring, as she always did, deeds above words, she founded the Distress Fund for South African Women and Children, and sailed for South Africa, persuading the authorities to permit her to make an inspection of the British concentration camps.[x] Of the conditions she discovered there, she wrote: 'I call this camp system a wholesale cruelty. To keep these camps going is to murder the children.' There were those within the authorities whom she considered to 'do their best with very limited means', but this was 'all only a miserable patch on a great ill'. She had encountered, with terrible clarity, the faceless power of the machinery of state evil, against which individual acts of moral courage can seem to count almost for nothing.

Her report on camp conditions was delivered to the British Government in 1901. 'Above all', she wrote, 'one would hope that the good sense, if not the mercy, of the English people will cry out against the further development of this cruel system which falls with such crushing effect upon the old, the weak, and the children.' In response to her report a formal commission was formed, and official investigators – led by Millicent Fawcett – were sent to make further inspections of the camps. But the quality of English mercy was strained: on the last Sunday before Christmas in 1901 Mr Charles Aked, a Baptist minister, gave a sermon in which he explicitly deplored 'a cowardly war ... conducted by methods of barbarism – the concentration camps have been murder camps'. The congregation was moved more to anger than to pity, and after the service the preacher was followed home by a vengeful crowd, and the windows of his house were broken. When a photograph emerged of the seven-year-old Lizzie van Zyl, dying of typhus in the camp at Bloemfontein, Arthur Conan Doyle surmised that this was proof not of British malignity, but of criminal neglect on the part of a Boer mother (Emily, undaunted, made her investigations; and having identified the photographer was able to exculpate the mother entirely). In her work *The Brunt of War and Where it Fell*, Emily wrote:

> Efforts to nullify the effect of my story, lest public sentiment should be aroused, took two forms, viz. criticism of myself and justification of the camps. I was labelled 'a political agitator', a 'disseminator of inaccurate and blood-curdling stories'.

Nevertheless, the work of Emily Hobhouse and the Fawcett Commission had its effects. By the end of 1901 there were no new inmates at the camps, and orders were made to mitigate the death rate – but not for the imprisoned Black population, for whom improvements were delayed, and scant.

Rebecca Solnit, writing of the moment Pandora opened her jar and loosed the world's ills, reminds the reader that to live in ignorance of those ills is not to live a whole life. 'Adam and Eve', she says, 'eat from the Tree of Knowledge and they are never ignorant again. (Some ancient cultures thanked Eve for making us fully human and conscious.)' Emily Hobhouse had been Pandora, loosing the lid of the jar, bringing concealed ills to light, to the discomfort and horror of those who would have much preferred to seal the vessel with wax. She said, 'Crass male ignorance, helplessness and muddling … I rub salt into the sore places in their minds, because it is good for them.'

Late in life, drowsing in her cottage by the sea, still containing inside her body the dauntless traveller she had been, Emily keenly felt the loss of her reputation. On

1 May 1926, she wrote to her friend Tibbie Steyn:

> ... though it is the late hour and little of life remains in me, I do feel some sort of re-institution in the public mind of England and documentary evidence of it, would do more than anything else to brighten the remaining time.

One month and one week later, having left East Wittering for London, she died. Her death was not reported in the British press; neither mourners nor clergymen attended her cremation in Golders Green. A man who'd never known her signed the register *J. Baker*, and put the wooden casket containing her ashes on the train to Southampton. These ashes are now buried in the base of the National Women's Monument in Bloemfontein,[xi] which commemorates the 27,000 women and children who died in the British concentration camps. Its central image is that of a Boer woman cradling an emaciated child, created by the sculptor Anton van Wouw thirteen years previously, and based on a description given by Emily of a dying child she had encountered during her investigations in the camps. Never much minded to applaud the works of men, she wrote that it would perhaps have been a more accurate representation of suffering, 'had he seen it with his own eyes'.

8

IN THE SUMMER of 2019, in Harriet Martineau's home town of Norwich where I now live, a number of unofficial blue plaques appeared all over the city, fixed to various buildings. These were installed by Rosie's Plaques – women of the Common Lot theatre company – to commemorate women whom history had not taken into account. Visitors to Norwich Castle were invited to remember Emma de Gauder, Countess of Norfolk, who in 1075, and at the age of sixteen, defended the keep against the king; elsewhere there was a memorial to Mabel Clarkson, the city's first woman councillor, and – as the plaque remarks – the 'first of many; still too few'. Down by Fye Bridge on the River Wensum, where there'd once been a ducking-stool to torment suspected witches, a plaque was dedicated to the memory of 'the unknown women' who had been burned or hanged: it said, 'we will not be silent'.

A further plaque was fixed to what had once been Norwich's Quaker Meeting House, and this is where I'd gather my Essex girl ghosts, if I could bring them up by bus from the Chelmsford hospital grounds, with Kim Kardashian and Gemma Collins gossiping in the back seat. I'd see Anne Knight standing there, handing pamphlets out to bewildered passersby; I'd see Rose Allin, carrying her jug, indifferent to the burn on her hand; and Harriet Martineau, offering her arm to Emily Hobhouse, each explaining by turns what they have done, and what they have seen: 'I said that I should do it all the same.' They are the Essex girl territory, and not the map. They are what it means to be disreputable, disrespectful, disobedient; to speak out of turn, and too loudly, and too often; to be irritable and irritating; to be bodies which are distasteful and inconvenient; to be a thorn in the flesh of the established and the ruling classes; to be at liberty. They have made it possible for me to understand that the Essex girl is not an identity to be despised and disavowed, but to be admired and imitated – regardless, in fact, of birthplace or gender; that those who resist the obligation to 'keep the varnish of the reputation fresh' may well go on to resist all the obligations imposed on them. Above my assembled Essex ghosts, on the wall of the meeting house where I imagine they stand looking steadily at me, the blue plaque reads as follows:

DEDICATED TO THE PROFANE
AND OPINIONATED WOMEN
WHO GATHERED HERE

NOTES

i Princess Dinubolu was the subject of the film *Forgotten Black Essex* (2018), made by the Southend-based artist Elsa James, working with historian Steve Martin. The Senegalese beauty attributed the remarkable softness of her skin to a habit of burying herself up to the neck in the sand at Yarmouth Beach, a claim which may well have been a justifiable prank on the locals.

ii In an interview with the *Observer* in May 2020, the political journalist and commentator Beth Rigby – an Essex girl, born in Colchester – said, 'I thought I'd posh-ed up my accent when I went to Cambridge. But then I joined the *FT*, and I realised that I really hadn't. A colleague, who was very posh, took the mickey out of the fact that I can't pronounce my Gs. I was absolutely crushed. For a while, it really affected my confidence. At Sky, I had a conversation with one of my bosses. "Shall we fix this?" I asked. They said: "Do you *want* to fix it?" I thought: no, actually, I don't. This is who I am.'

iii In her biography of George Eliot, the historian Kathryn Hughes describes Martineau – not, I think, without a faint suggestion of dislike – as 'plain, gauche and gossipy', and one whose 'old-maidish respectability ran alongside a prurient interest in other people's doings'. 'Hans Christian Anderson', she writes, 'once met her at a garden party in London, and was so exhausted by the experience that he had to go and lie down afterwards.'

iv In *Encounters with Harriet Martineau: A Victorian Living Ahead of her Time* (2017), Stuart Hobday writes that 'She seems to have been deliberately written out of history, which calls into question the nature of how history is remembered and recorded, the power of myth-making and why some things are deemed relevant and others not. Martineau had two important qualifications that led to her dismissal by the later 19th-century male establishment: she was an intellectual woman and also became widely known as an atheist.'

v Matthew Hopkins is commonly understood to have been a Puritan, and Puritans are commonly understood to have been the motivating force behind the witch trials. But a belief in the literal presence of demons and malign spirits was not confined to Puritanism, and in fact where Puritan scholars addressed the matter directly it was often with a profound unease. The Essex Puritan minister George Gifford, who published two works on witchcraft, believed the fear of 'cunning men and women' to be purely a spiritual matter, to be dealt with by prayer, and not ducking-stools and pyres in the town square. Nor, as an aside, were Puritans especially puritanical where sex is concerned: a good deal of Puritan writing urges couples – albeit ones decently wed – to, as one anonymous preacher put it, 'joyfully give due benevolence one to the other; as two musical instruments rightly fitted do make a most pleasant and sweet harmony in a well-tuned consort.'

vi Copies of *The Acts and Monuments* were ordered to be placed in churches alongside the King James Bible, and noble families were instructed to ensure copies were available for the edification of the household staff. It began to affirm a kind of English exceptionalism: of a valiant indomitable island nation, mercifully severed from the continent by water, and free from the Catholic Church – but free only for the moment, and never to rest easy, but to be alert to the merest whiff of Popish incense drifting across the Channel. I do not think it is entirely fanciful to suggest that the outcome of the Brexit Referendum in 2016 was influenced – however unconsciously, and however dissipated by the passage of time – by the work of John Foxe.

vii By December 2019, the UK government had closed 800 public libraries since 2010.

viii By way of context, it should be noted that Anne Knight's travels took place eight years after the publication, in 1817, of *Persuasion* by Jane Austen, whose fiction has done so much to form the contemporary image of women in the first part of the nineteenth century. But Anne Knight was both exceptional and typical. In an article in the *Quaker History Journal* in 1982, Gail Malmgreen writes: 'Even in the heyday of Victorian feminine and domestic ideals a determined single woman (always assuming that she had some small income of her own) could find a haven in hotels, apartments, and lodging-houses frequented by co-thinkers ... if sufficiently healthy and intrepid she could travel, even unaccompanied, and she could speak in public, attend meetings and conferences, and build her own circle of acquaintance.'

ix It would appear to have been a point of pride on the part of Emily Hobhouse to be physically strong. In *To Love One's Enemies: The Work and Life of Emily Hobhouse* (1994), Jennifer Hobhouse Balme writes that 'Emily, being the youngest [of her sisters], was determined to keep up with the other two, a tenacity which she showed when, in a game of shuttlecock and battledore – a type of badminton – she and her father's curate kept a rally going for two thousand strokes, a feat that lasted two hours.'

x In January 2019, during an episode of *Question Time* on the BBC, the then British government minister Jacob Rees-Mogg suggested that the British internment camps during the Boer war had been a wholly humanitarian effort on the part of the British, designed to feed and house Boer women and children while the men of what was largely a farming community were occupied in the war. In fact, though the British camps had initially been designed to house, for the duration of the war, the 'Protected Burghers' who had made pledges of neutrality, in the three years from 1899 approximately

48,000 people died in what had become concentration camps. Of the 28,000 deaths of white Boers, 22,000 were children. Of the Black population imprisoned there, no proper record was taken of the child mortality rate, but it is estimated to be 80 per cent. In response to the *Question Time* episode, the novelist Damian Barr sent Rees-Mogg a copy of his novel *You Will Be Safe Here*, which is set in a Boer concentration camp, and through which I first met Emily Hobhouse.

xi The National Women's Monument is the largest memorial to Emily Hobhouse, but by no means the only. Roads, towns and university campuses bear her name, and in 1968 a French-built Daphné class submarine was christened the *SAS Emily Hobhouse*. In 1994, with the end of apartheid, when all naval vessels bearing European names were renamed, the submarine became the *SAS Umkhonto*, this being the Zulu word for 'spear'.

LIST OF ILLUSTRATIONS

SELECT BIBLIOGRAPHY

Elsabé Brits, *Emily Hobhouse: Beloved Traitor* (Cape Town, Tafelberg, 2016).

John Foxe, *Foxe's Book of Martyrs: Select Narratives* (Oxford, Oxford World's Classics, 2009).

Stuart Hobday, *Encounters with Harriet Martineau* (London, Unbound, 2017).

Emily Hobhouse, *The Brunt of War, and Where it Fell* (First published 1902).

Richard Holloway, *Godless Morality: Keeping Religion Out of Ethics* (Edinburgh, Canongate, 2004).

Audre Lorde, *The Cancer Journals* (London, Penguin Classics, 2020).

Harriet Martineau, *Life in the Sick-Room: Essays* (First published 1844).

Rebecca Solnit, *Men Explain Things to Me* (London, Granta, 2014).

ACKNOWLEDGEMENTS

This book is based on the Harriet Martineau lecture which I gave in 2018 as part of the Norfolk and Norwich Festival, on the invitation of the National Centre for Writing.

I am grateful to my parents, David and Maureen Butler, and my husband, Robert Perry, for their assistance with this book as in all things. Thank you for Rose Allin, Mr Ashdown. Thank you to Chris Gribble, Stuart Hobday, Rebecca Rideal, and Damian Barr. Thank you to my friends. Thank you, again and as ever, to Jenny Hewson, Hannah Westland and Emily Berry; and to all at Lutyens & Rubinstein and at Serpent's Tail.